THE 99%
WOMAN

"A guide that unlocks the secrets for embracing yourself as a whole woman who attracts more love, financial freedom and success!"

THE 99% WOMAN

"A guide that unlocks the secrets for embracing yourself as a whole woman who attracts more love, financial freedom and success!"

DARRYL S. BRISTER

Tyza Brister
Book Coordinator
1937 Mirabeau Ave.
New Orleans, LA 70122

Ordering Information:
Quantity sales. Special discounts are available on quantity purchases by corporations, associations, and others. For details, contact the publisher at the address above.
Orders by U.S. trade bookstores and wholesalers.

Follow Darryl S. Brister:
email: bishopbristerbooks@gmail.com
Facebook: https://facebook.com/bishopdsbrister
Instagram: instagram.com/bishopdsbrister
Periscope: https://periscope.tv/bishopdsbrister
YouTube: https://www.youtube.com/user/DSBministries
Twitter: https://www.twitter.com/bishopdsbrister
Website: http://beaconlight.org/our-pastor

ISBN: 978-0-578-67263-2

Also by Darryl S. Brister

* * *

Exposing the Enemy
The Monster Within
Recovering from Ruptured Relationships
Don't Fight the Process
Talk to Me Afterwards
Look to the Hills
Living the Dream
Doing Right In A Wrong World
Against All Odds: Turning Obstacles Into Opportunities

Dedication

This book is dedicated to:

My Wife
Dr. Dionne Flot Brister

My 5 Sisters
Sandra Dorsey, Dorothy Holmes, Julia Oubré, Diane Owens, and Gwendolyn Reed

My 3 Daughters
Darrlynn Brister Alston, Dariel Brister Francois, and Tyza Devell Brister

My 2 Granddaughters
Emersyn Joy Francois & Gracyn Joy Francois

My Spiritual Mothers
Pastor Debra B. Morton, Lady Catherine Raphael, and Pastor Valerie I. Holcomb

Lastly, a special dedication to the Mothers of Beacon Light International Baptist Cathedral

Mother Janie Malveaux
Mother Claudette Early
Mother Sadie Harrell
Mother Stephanie Jones
Mother Sue Johnson
Mother Willie Deal
Mother Carolyn Arceneaux
Mother Cora Sandifer
Mother Cherry Lockett
Mother Effie Banks
Mother Emily Braneon
Mother Jerlene Bridges
Mother Ezeal Thomas
Mother Loretta Joseph
Mother Glenda Knox
Mother Constance Favorite
Mother Carrie Jones

Author Bio

Darryl Sylvester Brister is the Second Presiding Bishop of the Full Gospel Baptist Church Fellowship International, Apostle/Overseer of Beacon Light International Ministries, and Senior Pastor/Teacher of Beacon Light International Baptist Cathedral in New Orleans, Louisiana.

Bishop Brister has ministered the Word of God in several countries such as Japan, Holland, Panama, Korea, Iceland, Africa, Trinidad, Tortola, and Europe. He attended Louisiana State University and later honorably served his country as a soldier in the United States Army. He received a Bachelor of Theology Degree from McKinley Theological Seminary, a Masters of Arts in Biblical Studies, a Doctorate of Ministry and a Doctorate of Philosophy in Religious Studies from Friends International Christian University.

Bishop Brister has received numerous awards and his leadership ability has been recognized throughout the world. He was inducted into the Morehouse College Martin Luther King Jr. Board of Preachers. He was also featured in Ebony Magazine as one of the Top 50 Leaders of Tomorrow,

Upscale Magazine's Millennium Tribute to America's Most Outstanding Pastors, Gospel Today as one of The World's Most Loved Pastors, and the New Orleans City Business Success Guide. Bishop Brister has also been featured in the Who's Who of Houston, Texas and was featured on the cover of an edition of Epitome Magazine.

Bishop Brister has made an impact as a speaker, teacher and prayer warrior in whatever environment he has stepped into from the ghetto of uptown New Orleans to the White House of this nation. He still possesses the unique ability to capture and connect with others whether it is The Premier of the British Virgin Islands, the Honorable Andrew Fahie; leaders of corporate companies like Chick-fil-A; or a passerby from his old stomping grounds in New Orleans.

He serves as President and Founder of the Darryl S. Brister Bible College and Theological Seminary, and is the Founder of the former Beacon Light Christian Academy. Bishop Brister has authored nine books that have ministered to thousands.

He is married to Dionne Flot Brister and is the father of five children and 3 grandchildren.

He is the Apostle/Overseer of a family of churches in Louisiana, Florida and Texas:

Beacon Light Baptist Church of Houma, Louisiana
Beacon Light Baptist Church of Hammond, Louisiana
Beacon Light of Hammond (Livingston Campus), Louisiana
Beacon Light Baptist Church of Baton Rouge, Louisiana
Beacon Light of Haiti at New Orleans, Louisiana
Beacon Light of Laplace, Louisiana
Beacon Light Community Church of Panama City, Florida
Believe Church of Houston, Texas

Contents

Introduction

I wrote this book with my mother in mind. She was my God-given angel on earth up until the day she passed away on September 20, 2017. This was just shy of her 94th birthday. She had just the right dose of humanity that made her a 99% woman. Even with such a beautiful and strong role model, I wondered how I would put into words the characteristics that capture the essence of a woman.

As a woman, you have a sacred role and a royal calling. You hold a place in the lives of men and children that is inimitable, irreplaceable and most certainly, irrevocable. Governments and kingdoms have flourished under your leadership, while many a great man has fallen for the love of an equally great woman, much like yourself. Children have been nurtured and guided to greatness under your skilled hands and careful eye.

God says your price is far above rubies.

Although many men from around the world gladly stand, clap, and agree, society still struggles to fully appreciate your value and contributions. You often fight against stigmas, policies and systems that wish to subdue you, limit your power and influence, and silence your voice. Many women, like you, have been mis-educated regarding your greatness, potential, and identity in Christ. I seek to change that.

Like my own mother, you are an amazing woman who, with just the right bit of information, can gain the edge required in order to cross over into 100% wholeness. This book will be the first of many that will help you break chains and ceilings that have been imposed on you by society. I also want to help you uncover and come against the lies you often unknowingly believe about yourself. In the following pages, you will learn:

> ➢ How to take what you have and turn it into your success advantage.
> ➢ Mindset secrets that will push you from "just getting by" to excellence.
> ➢ Information about yourself and the dating game that will ensure you never settle for crumbs again.
> ➢ The tools for attracting money and opportunities into your life.
> ➢ Affirmations that reinforce your learning and challenge you to go deeper for a total transformation.
> ➢ … And more!

To get the most out of this book, keep a pen and journal with you to document your journey and write down fresh insights and personal reflections. You'll be surprised at how much your self-awareness about who you are as a whole woman increases. So please don't rush through the chapters. Your goal is not to simply "finish" reading the book, but to apply what you learn about yourself.

Throughout this book, I freely share the successes and setbacks other women have experienced. The purpose of each story is to help you relate to the hidden lessons. It's important that you learn from other women who have lost sight of their identity, so that it doesn't happen (or continue to happen) to you. Remember, God has given you everything you need in order to experience unlimited levels of success, relationship satisfaction, and financial freedom. The key to accessing what God promises lies in your willingness to do the hard work of overcoming false beliefs, mindset traps, and lack of knowledge. You are a phenomenal 99% woman, but this year, I consider it my greatest honor to welcome you to the 100% club.

"The only limit to the height of your achievements is the reach of your dreams and your willingness to work hard for them."
-Michelle Obama

Chapter 1

YOU HAVE WHAT IT TAKES TO SUCCEED

There's just something about former First Lady of the United States, Michelle Obama. It's in the way she holds her shoulders and the tilt of her chin. She isn't the boldest or loudest voice in the room. However, when she opens her mouth to speak about her passion, you feel that she's a woman that gets things done. And she does. She consistently achieves success and prosperity as she defines it.

You see, success isn't something that I can define for someone else because what is important for me may not matter much to you. For example, I know a woman whose idea of success is to raise healthy children who value education and a relationship with Jesus as deeply as she does. Yet another young lady I know has a dream of having a business that produces multiple streams of 7-figure income each year. Another woman in her 80s defines success as loving and supporting her husband and furthering his legacy.

How do you define success? I can't create your definition of success, but I will share characteristics you have in common with other successful women. As you read through the list, know that I am describing you. The real you. You are a successful woman. God says, "you are fearfully and wonderfully made" (Psalm 139:141). Although greatness is already within you, learning and implementing foundational principles serves to sharpen you. There's an old saying, "A sharp knife always cuts better than a dull one." So, make a note of where you see yourself and also where you may need to strengthen some of the characteristics listed below.

1. You're Spiritual

We all know or have heard of highly successful women who do not have a relationship with Jesus, nor do they put God first. This book wasn't written to bash these women or deny that success via the world's means isn't possible. However,

I've been walking with the Lord for over 30 years and I have at least a few stories about times when I tried to do my own thing. Believe me when I say God can open doors no man can shut. He calls you qualified when on paper you should be denied. God makes a way when there appears to be no way and during those times when I've been fed up, burned out, shut in, and experiencing a downturn, He strengthened me! I'm a living witness that "I can do all things through Christ who gives me strength" (Philippians 4:13). I have countless stories of others who have experienced the same! When you weigh the benefits of a life with Christ, many people loudly agree that it just doesn't make sense to build a life without Him. Here's a story to illustrate my point.

Story of the Three Sons

There were three sons from an affluent family in a large metropolitan city. Their father had expanded the huge empire built by the grandfather. The family had a great reputation and were quite powerful. When the first son mentioned his father's name, a flood of investors financed his business ventures and he became very wealthy within seven years. The second son mentioned his father's name and he received referrals from high level business leaders and he gained access to an exclusive school and membership club. He became an in-demand attorney serving the city's high society. The third son moved to another state and paved his own way. Pride made him want to prove that he could do it on his own. It took 23 years, but he made it. He built a solid business, but his children and grandchildren would never have the far-reaching impact, influence, prosperity, access or support that his brothers and their families enjoyed.

The moral of the story is to enjoy the full, immeasurable spiritual, financial and health benefits that come when your Father is the King! Re-creating the wheel is not a wise strategy and as a successful woman, you deserve the fullness of life. Keep God first!

2. You're an Overcomer

Life may or may not have knocked you around a few times, but you've learned how to fight back. You don't expect life to be fair. Although you haven't always known how you will make it through the challenges you face, you just know you will. You have both hope and faith. The hope keeps you believing in a brighter future. The faith keeps you moving forward and doing the required work, even when times may be hard.

Shantae was a single mother who escaped an abusive marriage to keep her children from harm. She also had an abusive childhood. She was an entrepreneur and although she made a high annual income, there were times when she went longer than 60 days without a sale. One month, money was so tight, Shantae had to hide her car to avoid repossession. During these dry spells, she sometimes didn't know where the family's next meal would come from. Sure, she felt discouraged and even afraid many times, but with God and supportive friends, Shantae always persevered. She felt the fear and still made the sales calls and showed up to do the hard work, even if that meant she did so from the comfort of her bed! This is a woman who spent a lot of time in prayer. There were moments when positive thoughts failed her. However, she never stopped believing that she would get on the other side of the problem she faced. And she did!

3. You Have a Vision

The Lord tells us to "Write the vision, and make it plain on tablets, that he who runs may read it" (Habakkuk 2:2). A woman who has goals also has a vision. A vision is the ability to see or believe in a preferred future. You are the type of woman who sees your future and has clarity about how to achieve it.

Rachel Hollis is an author, speaker, and entrepreneur who dreamed of speaking in front of tens of thousands of women. She wrote down her vision and put pictures of her goals on a vision board. She prayed about them, wrote her vision, and looked at her board every single day. She wrote her first book and sold a few copies. She wrote her second, third, fourth and fifth books. None really "blew up" the way she had hoped. She kept praying and visualizing and reminding herself of her vision. Her sixth book hit the *New York Times* Best Sellers List and eventually moved into the #1 spot. Her seventh book is in the #2 spot! She is one of *Inc's* Top 30 Entrepreneurs Under 30 and speaks to sold out crowds all over the world. At the time of this writing, this powerhouse of a young lady said that most of her social media followers have only become aware of her over the last three months! Rachel has been hustling and dreaming every day for 15 years before her vision came to life. Yet, today, she is literally living her dreams. The key here is in having more than just a good idea. As a successful woman, you possess a true vision with a passion to match. We'll discuss visualization and goal getting in more detail in chapter four.

4. You're Confident

Your confidence doesn't mean you never experience insecurity or fear. As a success-minded woman, you have the courage to take action despite your insecurities or fears. You don't fuel negative emotions by comparing yourself to others or by listening to people who don't believe in you. You are confident in your skills, knowledge and abilities. This doesn't mean you know everything, but you know you can and will figure it out. You have a positive attitude and an optimistic outlook on life. Your gift is found in your ability to focus on the areas in which you are strong. This serves to increase your confidence!

Simone Biles is an Olympic gymnast and the most decorated athlete in the world. Here is what she has to say about confidence. There was a time Simone was so distraught about mistakes she made during competition that she couldn't face off against her opponents in the vault event. She sought out a sports psychologist who helped her develop coping skills for dealing with the pressure that comes with performance anxiety. She went on to become a gold medalist in the event. The International Gymnastics Federation even named a vault maneuver after Biles. Simone's name will live forever because she overcame her fears and developed confidence. Biles said, "I can only control what I do, not what anyone else wants me to do."

Preparation is everything! Practice your craft. Know as much as you can about the topic or area you are facing. When you know what you know, confidence shows up. Biles encourages readers to, "Be yourself, don't let anyone try to conform you to today's views, and have fun!" If you're having fun and being authentic, a confident posture is a natural result.

5. You Love Learning

There's a saying: "You can't pour from an empty vessel." Choosing to be a well-read woman increases the pool of information you have available. You are well aware that you can't implement a solution you don't know about! I know a mom who was raised in a family where her parents were very religious and judgmental towards her and others. She grew up believing that everyone who did not share her religious background would burn in hell. While her first child was still a baby, she decided not to raise a family with those same values and beliefs. She began studying child rearing. She researched books from the early 1900s to the present day. This mom read, watched videos, and studied successful moms to learn how to move past whoopings and yelling at her kids in order to use discipline with intention. She learned to teach her children morals and godly values through the telling of Bible stories. It's no surprise that everywhere she goes, people compliment her on her four children.

The success-minded woman, like you, soars because you're eager to learn about what interests you. You are open to new concepts and ideas on money management, relationship dynamics, communication, different business types, current events, the things of God, hobbies, health and wellness, femininity, and more. You study "to show thyself approved" (2 Tim. 2:15). Researchers have found that the brains of people who consistently seek out learning opportunities actually create new neural pathways. That means the brain's capacity can increase. If you don't believe me, Google it! Study something new and keep filling your "cup!"

6. You're Connected to Others

As a successful woman, you know important it is to depend on other people and build relevant relationships. Finishing strong in this life is often a team sport. Let's look to high level athletes for an example of this.

In "solo" races like long-distance running and biking, winning is still a team effort. In a bike race, the team leader is chosen and her teammates do everything possible to help her win. They ride in front of the leader to shield her from the wind and to create a formation that blocks rival athletes from taking the lead. They chase down rival riders and take turns holding the pace while the leader conserves energy. The team leader makes the final sprint to the finish and shares her cash prize with the team who supported her. The same is true for you. Although there aren't first, second or third place finishers in the game of life, you want to surround yourself with a team that is headed in the same direction.

You want people in your life who can carry the load, have your back, and encourage you when the wind picks up and the uphill climb gets hard. This is a group of people who are striving for success and who share a similar trajectory. Your peers provide encouragement, accountability, and support for the ups and downs that are sure to come. Sometimes peers are very close friends, sometimes not.

Recently, an elected official in her early 40s shared how she retired from the U.S. Army, won a local election, and launched a growing non-profit organization that serves women veterans – all in one year! She attributes her rapid growth to commitment to God's plan for her life and also having a group of positive women who fast and pray together. "For where two or three are gathered together in my name, there I am in the midst of them" (Matthew 19:20).

As a successful woman, you also deserve to have a mentor. The mentor is someone who provides insights needed to achieve the "next level." In this age of social media, businesses can also benefit greatly from joint ventures and referrals formed through collaborations. As a success-minded woman, you seek out connections with the intention of giving and receiving value. It isn't a one-sided relationship where you only look out for yourself, nor are you over-giving to a point where you feel drained and exhausted. Although you match the energy of others, you also have the wisdom to know that serving a mentor is priceless.

Mentors and peers are crucial. Ideally, you will also have someone to sow into. Doing so aligns you with the spiritual law, "we also reap what we sow" (Galatians 6:7).

There are other attributes that you have in common with other success-minded women, and most important among these is your willingness to overcome limiting beliefs. Stay willing to overcome your internal limitations so you can become all you, and God, desire. This is so critical to success that I dedicated the next chapter to the topic.

Go Deeper

1. After reading through this chapter, what characteristics would you like to further develop in yourself? List them in your journal.

2. A mentor selects you, not the other way around. But a mentor will not notice you if you aren't doing something they can help you expand. What is one thing you can do today that makes a difference in the lives of others? How will you sustain it?

3. What is your vision? Write it down in great detail. Find a goal planning journal or Google an article that will help you plot goals and tasks that will bring clarity to how you will make your vision tangible.

4. Commit to increasing your learning and enhancing your spiritual self. Every Friday at 6 a.m. Central, my wife, Lady Brister, and I do a live broadcast on Facebook (facebook.com/BishopDSBrister) and Instagram (@BishopDSBrister). Pause now and follow my pages so you can get these weekly spiritual deposits in addition to your daily study.

"I am responsible for every result in my life. If I want different results, I have to change my thoughts and actions."

Chapter 2

GET YOUR MIND RIGHT

It's commonly said, "God wants us to be emotionally whole." I want to take this a step further and insist that God requires emotional wholeness. It's a prerequisite to having all that He promises. It is also true that faith and hope are also key components. In my decades of counseling women, I find that brokenness, past hurts, traumas, and negative mindsets hinder the ability to believe and receive. So really, one of the most prevalent roadblocks to wholeness and faith activation is not being able to identify the traits or habits that contribute to brokenness. I want to tell you three things that will make a significant difference in helping you become whole. If you can take these three things and decide to use them, your life will change, starting today.

1. Learn to Control Emotions

One way to become emotionally whole is to learn how to control your emotions. There are at least six different psychological theories that describe and explain the number and purpose of emotions, so we don't know everything on the subject. But one thing we do know is that emotions influence our thoughts and behaviors. Our goal as Christians is to control our emotions so that we may build up others and ourselves. Too often, however, we allow our emotions to control us, forcing us to make decisions that we regret later. For example, an insecure woman is often motivated and influenced by a strong desire to be accepted and liked. In her quest to gain acceptance, she tends to "go along with" others' agendas at her job and in her intimate relationships that may not benefit her. She wants to avoid feeling the pain of loss. She can't bear disapproval or rejection, so she finds herself in situations where she is trying to impress people she may not even actually like!

It is normal to have an emotional reaction to a situation. Problems only develop when you lose control of your thoughts and behavior because of the emotion. My wife and I have a spiritual daughter who, years ago, was dating and looking for Mr. Right. After her dates, something like this consistently occurred: she was usually very optimistic about the future between the two of them. She would text and talk about him to her closest friends. After a few dates, she started wondering aloud if he could be "the one." Of course, she didn't share her thoughts with the man, but there was an excitement about the possibilities. She would already have started falling in love because of the way he treated her.

Then, it would happen. One day, he didn't text as frequently or maybe something came up at work. She would assume the worst. She was certain he was blowing her off, cheating, or was a player. So, she would send these long, detailed texts, which included ultimatums. She would eventually delete and block the guy and write him off as "another no-good man."

Our spiritual daughter was probably a lot like some of you reading this book. Smart, capable, caring and genuine. Yet, you find yourselves in the same emotional cycle. The key to breaking this type of cycle is identifying where your emotions have taken center place and where your logic would serve you best. Earlier I mentioned a lot of you are stuck in a place of brokenness because you have not identified the emotions and experiences that hold you back. Let's break this down.

In the scenario I shared above, our spiritual daughter interpreted her dating experience to mean something different from what it should have meant. Excitement after a date is better interpreted as, "Wow, I had a great time!" But that is all it should mean. She could have used that information to decide whether she wanted a second date. Instead, she interpreted her euphoria as, "Wow, I could really possibly have a future with this guy!"

When the guy wasn't texting as frequently, her brokenness from past events started to come through. She felt emotions related to grief, loss and rejection. If she were coming from a place of wholeness, she would have been busy going on second dates with other qualified men. She wouldn't have taken his texting frequency in a negative way. Instead of feeling grief or rejection, she would have probably drawn a more positive conclusion like, "He must be swamped with work."

The young lady unknowingly added pressure and expectations to her budding relationships because she didn't see how unresolved grief and issues from past relationships (a.k.a. brokenness) caused her to jump to unfair conclusions. How many times have you ended a phone call in anger without saying goodbye, quit a job or relationship, left a church, showed out, or hurt someone else due to runaway emotions? As you can see, controlling your emotions is a necessary life skill. When our emotions are messed up, our judgments are messed up.

2. Identify the Emotions that Keep You Broken

The first thing you want to do is identify common emotions that generally keep people in a broken state and reflect on the scenarios that stir any of those emotions up inside of you. Study your own thoughts and behaviors and write down what you learn about yourself. In this chapter, I will discuss three emotions that seem to impact a lot of the women I counsel. These are loneliness, fear, and desire. Ironically, these three emotions surface in the first three chapters of Genesis.

In the beginning, God created the earth, animals, and a man. The man said something was still missing. He needed a companion. We could say Adam got lonely. "The Lord God said, it is not good that man should be alone. I will make him a helper comparable to him." Here, God expresses not only the importance of, but he also hints at the importance of being equally yoked with your companion. When Adam and Eve disobeyed God by eating from the fruit of the tree in the midst of the garden (desire), they hid themselves from the presence of the Lord God. Here, the concept of fear is introduced (Genesis 1:26; 2:18).

Desire, loneliness, and fear aren't negative emotions simply because they show up in your soul. It is when we allow these emotions to reign over our will that they become destructive and cause us to sin. Emotions are meant to serve us, not master us. Never allow negative emotions to reign over your will. Here's what that looks like.

Loneliness can be rooted in childhood issues like divorced or absentee parents, failed relationships, lack of friendships or a social group. Sometimes loneliness is coming from a deeper place within you, so you have to take responsibility for bringing that to the surface and ask God to heal it. Desire can be the underlying cause of envy, jealousy, lust, gluttony, ungratefulness, griping, gossiping, being a "hater" or a "Negative Nancy."

Maybe you fill your mind with images and stories (think Instagram and television) that make you want material things, a lifestyle, or a mate you haven't yet put in the work to receive. You want something you feel you can't have or aren't qualified to have. This mindset is a trick of the enemy because God says you are already qualified. Yes, there may be additional moves you need to make in order to access what belongs to you, but the wrong focus can delay the manifestation of the promise.

Fear is the emotion that keeps a person feeling frozen. This is when you are afraid to take the risks required to advance your life. So how can you know if you are operating from a place of fear? Look for behaviors like procrastination, laziness, and lack of motivation. Left unchecked, fearfulness can become a lifestyle. As a success-minded woman, you certainly don't have time for that!

3. Replace Negative Emotions with Positive Ones

In order to overcome a negative mindset, look for ways to accentuate positive emotions. Just as there are negative emotions, there are also positive ones. Positive emotions were given so that God can live through us.

In Galatians 5:22-23, nine positive emotions are identified. We have love, joy, peace, long suffering, kindness, goodness, faithfulness, gentleness, and self-control. Against such, there is no law. We should practice displaying these emotions every day. Here's a daily practice that will help you remember the positive emotions you are committed to developing. First, keep reading about the different positive states in the Bible. Physically touch yourself and say, "Lord, make me whole." Then accentuate positive emotions. Here's how to do that.

I recommend using the Word of God to identify the emotions you want more of in your life. "For the word of God is living and powerful and sharper than any two-edged sword, piercing even to the division of soul and spirit and of joints and marrow and is a discerner of thoughts and intents of the heart" (Hebrews 4:12). Make a list of the positive emotions listed above. Then under each one, imagine a moment or experience that made you feel that emotion. If it is hard to think of moments from your life, browse the Internet and search for stories about love, peace, kindness, etc. You can even reflect on a movie or TV show you watched, or imagine an experience you would like to have. You are only limited by the power of your imagination! So, dig in. Replacing negative thoughts and feelings is not easy, but with consistency and effort, it becomes easier. The Word of God will help you to become emotionally whole. You got this!

Go Deeper

1. Think about the last time you lost control of your emotions. Ask yourself why you chose to react in that way. Try to take full responsibility for your part in the event. Avoid saying, "I don't know," or "I did it because he/she was acting stupid!"

2. Make a list of the types of situations or interactions that stir up negative emotions like guilt, shame, fear, anxiety or uncontrolled anger.

3. Research 3-5 scriptures or Bible-based affirmations can you write down and meditate on each day to prepare your mind and spirit to make a more positive response to the next "triggering" situation.

"When I loved myself enough, I began leaving whatever wasn't healthy. This meant people, jobs, my own beliefs and habits – anything that kept me small. My judgement called it disloyal. Now I see it as self-loving."
– Kim McMillian

Chapter 3

FOUR SELF-LOVE TRAPS

Are you a person who smiles on the outside while hurting on the inside? If so, let's change that! In Chapter 2, we discussed how overcoming negative emotions is one way of becoming emotionally whole. Another way is to learn how to love yourself. But some people have such low self-esteem, they can't stand to look at themselves in the mirror. They despise their very existence and see themselves as being unworthy and inadequate. Although it is common to hear experts say, "Love yourself before you can love someone else." I disagree. Many women are struggling just to *like* themselves! Let's stop trying to skip to step three of a process when we haven't yet mastered the first step.

If we don't love ourselves, we accept subpar treatment from others. However, it is our boundaries that protect us from others' toxic behaviors. In order to embrace, create, and enforce healthy boundaries, we have to first know we are valuable and deserving of royal treatment. That knowledge is rooted in our feelings about ourselves (a.k.a. our self-image). Despite what some may believe, it is not necessary to become conceited and vain in order to have a positive self-image. In fact, people who see themselves as superior to others are just as emotionally unstable as people who see themselves as inferior.

As Christians, it is important for us to have a good self-image. When we have a good self-image, we are more willing to set and achieve goals, choose healthy relationships and make ourselves available to do the work of God. Feelings of unworthiness, insecurity, and self-doubt won't hinder us when we're whole! In this chapter, let's talk about the four self-love traps that destroy self-image, which then prevents you from liking yourself.

1. The Guilt Trap

Guilty feelings are normal and can help us remember to correct unwise behaviors. The healthy response to guilt is to acknowledge the wrong behavior, apologize if needed, and then move on. Guilt becomes toxic when you're consistently blaming yourself for things that aren't actually your fault and the feelings keep you weighed down under a growing mountain of guilt. Here are a few causes of guilt in our lives:

> ➢ Violating your morals and ethics
> ➢ Breaking a promise to yourself or others
> ➢ Hurting someone else
> ➢ Thinking ill will over someone
> ➢ Feeling like you "should have done more" for someone
> ➢ Being more successful than others
> ➢ Unrepented sin

Under the growing mountain of guilt, our self-image begins to disintegrate, and we become ineffective in our Christian mission. Therefore, to avoid the guilt trap, we must first confess our sins daily. Remind yourself that you are not your mistakes and that self-forgiveness is a must. Why? Because "There is therefore now no condemnation to them which are in Christ Jesus, who walk not after the flesh, but after the Spirit" (Romans 8:1).

When you face feelings of condemnation, guilt, and shame remember that those types of feelings block positivity, self-love, and love for others. Some people can feel so guilty they don't feel worthy to receive blessings, opportunities, or even forgiveness.

Have you ever been around someone who is constantly apologizing? How does that make you feel? You accidentally bump into them and they apologize to you before you can say anything. Or how about the person who keeps saying, "I'm sorry" over and over for things that weren't that serious or that should have been "water under the bridge?" Don't be that person!

We learned that in John 1:9, "If we confess our sins, He is faithful and just to forgive us our sins and to cleanse us from all unrighteousness." Believing this with all our heart, mind, and soul will help us to tear down that mountain of guilt and rebuild again. So even if you sincerely believe something is your fault, ask God to forgive you for it. If that feels impossible, don't be afraid to seek professional counsel.

2. The Overachievement Trap

A drive to reach goals and experience a high-level of success is a legitimate thing. However, there is such a thing as overachievement. There are people in this world who want to do everything themselves. They either don't trust anyone else to do it or they believe they are indispensable. At the root of overachievement is usually a belief that, "I'm not good enough." When a person doesn't feel good enough, they tend to overwork themselves in order to prove their value to others. The best way to feel good enough is to reaffirm who God says you are (see Ephesians 1-2).

Further, if you attempt to do everything yourself, you run the risk of exhaustion. When you collapse, you sometimes wake up to realize that you did not do everything you set out to do. You then become discouraged. Discouragement will destroy self-esteem. Can you see how overachievement leads to discouragement, which then damages self-esteem? In order to avoid discouragement, you must learn to break down large tasks into small steps that are easily achievable. A quick search on Amazon.com for a goal planner turned up more than 50,000 results! So there are resources available to help you figure out how to plan your life in a way that leads to success.

The concept I want you to take from here is that taking things step-by-step is one way to get clarity. Remember in chapter one, I shared insight about how clarity is critical for success? If you can't understand how to bring your vision to life, you won't ever see the fullness of it. Have you been working until the point of exhaustion only to just grab bits and pieces of your vision? No way! You want it all! So, get clarity and break your goals down into actionable steps.

Another habit overachievers usually have is they think they can't relax or slow down. I know several people who are always running, running, running. They can't just go to an appointment. They have to talk to one or two people on the phone while they're enroute. In the waiting room, they are texting, scrolling or doing something in order to get ahead. When someone is constantly trying to get ahead, it means they think they are behind. If this sounds familiar, what if I told you that you are right where you need to be at this particular point in your life? Each season has lessons that prepare us for the next season. You can't fall behind or get ahead, but you can become a fast learner!

You must learn how to strike a balance in your life. Make time for prayer, Bible study, and meditation. How can you identify hidden problem areas and break cycles, if you never slow down long enough to hear God's still, small voice?

3. The Criticism Trap

When it comes to criticism, you might be on the receiving end of it, or you could be the one who criticizes others. Both tendencies are unhealthy and indicate that low self-esteem is probably present. Let's talk about what happens when you receive a lot of criticism.

Criticism is expressing disapproval of someone based on "perceived" mistakes or faults. Years ago, I counseled a woman who was married to a man who was rarely satisfied by his wife's efforts. Whether she got her hair done or wore a new outfit, there was always something he found fault with. Sometimes, he offered a backhanded compliment where he would say, "That's such a gorgeous dress, but it's too tight around your back." Or he might say, "I love your hair! I think the color is a little off this time, don't you?" If he wasn't making comments like these, he was critiquing her cooking, cleaning, or even conversations he may have overheard. He might ask, "Why did you say it like that?" Or, "You shouldn't have said that to Ashley. Maybe you should have said XYZ instead."

As you can see, criticism can be a subtle act. It doesn't have to be a blatant insult like, "Wow, you got fat." Or "That's an awful color on you!" When you are in an environment where someone is consistently questioning your judgment, behavior, or appearance, it eventually causes you to doubt your own perceptions. Interacting with people who offer a steady flow of negative criticism damages self-esteem. Your strong and confident inner voice slowly becomes replaced with a critical voice.

Some people find that a poor opinion of self is often the result of wounds acquired during childhood. Maybe it's a mother, father, teacher, or pastor's critical voice pushing you down. Motivational speaker Les Brown shared a story about how when he was a child, the adults in his life told him he was learning disabled. They told him he couldn't do certain things because of the disability. He spent most of his school career believing self-limiting stories about himself. One day, a teacher he met in passing, told him to never say the words, "I can't" ever again. Les Brown went on to become an international celebrity, author, motivational speaker and serial entrepreneur.

Many of you are just like Les Brown used to be because you believe the lies spoken over you. As a result of constant criticism, one or more of the following false beliefs might feel true:

> I'm not good/smart/skilled/qualified enough
> I feel like I'm always in trouble/messing up
> I'm unattractive/ugly/overweight/skinny
> No one wants/loves/likes me

Thoughts like these are usually not completely true. Now, if there is a grain of truth in any of these statements (i.e. feeling unskilled or underqualified), keep reading because later in the book, I address ways to up level yourself to fit your future. Your thinking will follow!

People who listen to all criticism, and generally take it to heart, are a people who have a great need for other's approval. Remember, the only approval we need is the approval of Jesus Christ. His approval is not based on achievement or possessions, but on whether we are living according to His standards. A good rule to follow when considering whether someone's critique is valid would be to ask yourself: (1) Do they have the lifestyle and achievements you admire? (2) Do they have your best interest at heart? If you get a "NO!" response to both questions, then give their words less weight.

4. The Comparison Trap

There is the saying, if you compare yourself to others, you may become vain and bitter, for there will always be greater and lesser persons than yourself. If you see people who seem to have it all together, you may not be seeing all of who they are. One way to know if making comparisons is an area of weakness for you is to open your social media and notice how you feel when you look at photos in the following areas:

➤ Attractive couples
➤ Fit people posing or exercising
➤ Vacation or travel photos
➤ Photos of friends having fun together
➤ Photos of an attractive couple with beautiful children
➤ Women wearing luxury shoes, clothes or accessories
➤ Beautiful women

Maybe it doesn't bother you to look through a stranger's photos. But how do you react about the photos of women you know or follow who already have what you hope to have one day? If you find yourself feeling resentful, sour, or thinking things like, "Oh, I bet they are going broke to afford that!" "No one's really *that* happy." "She is doing too much!" or any other judgmental thought, check your heart. As Christians, we have to believe that when we are approved by God, the things that we want are on the way. If you look at someone's life and feel like you "measure up," you are more likely to feel good about yourself. But if you look over and feel like you don't, your self-esteem is likely to take a hit. I suggest you avoid following people and pages on social media that stir up negative feelings. Do it for yourself!

If you avoid the four traps that will destroy your self-image, you will begin to grow towards wholeness. Just as in other relationships, be kind to the "new you." When you avoid the four traps to a poor self-image, you might just fall in love with yourself!

Go Deeper

1. Which of the four traps seems to have you bound? Google a scripture that speaks to each one. Write it down and every morning and night, put your hand on your body and read it aloud until you believe it. In addition, each day say to yourself, "I love myself. I love me to life."

2. Who do you need to unfollow on social media in order to avoid making comparisons? Who do you need to spend less time with, in order to avoid criticism or guilty feelings? Make those necessary changes today!

"Every day, people settle for less than they deserve. They are only partially living or at best living a partial life. Every human being has the potential for greatness."
– Bo Bennett

Chapter 4

DON'T SETTLE FOR CRUMBS

Carmen's Story

Carmen bowed her head in embarrassment and shame as she thought about her failed relationships. A long time ago, she had lost count of the many men to whom she had given her heart, mind, and body. She remembered Jay and his chronic cheating before she got pregnant. He then ran off with her cousin.

Carmen thought about Mark who showered her with love and affection, only to be distant and moody later. This inconsistency went on for a year before he eventually stopped answering her calls. Then there was Karl who would never commit to marriage, nor would he define their six-year relationship. Antoine was married and swore he was going through a divorce. His lies felt like a hot knife in Carmen's heart.

Her hazel eyes peeked open to steal a glimpse at the therapist sitting on the couch across from her. She didn't want to be judged, but to Carmen's relief, Dr. Jules' eyes were filled with compassion. Carmen felt ready to ask the hard question. She was ready to stop being a victim and blaming these men for everything that happened. She took a deep breath and asked, "Dr. Jules, why do I keep settling for crumbs?"

Why Women Settle

Can you relate to any part of Carmen's story? In her relationships, Carmen often received resistance to important needs like:

- ➢ Emotional support
- ➢ Understanding
- ➢ A compassionate response

➢ A committed relationship
➢ Requests for reasonable changes

Repeatedly experiencing these types of responses caused her to question herself. She often wondered, "Am I asking for too much?" If you doubt whether your expectations for fair treatment are reasonable, you may have started to expect very little of yourself and others because you don't want to be "too much" for some people.

Sisters: fear is at the root of a willingness to make oneself appear smaller. But no longer do you deny yourself the treatment and things you really want for your life! You are a whole woman and the days of staying stuck, playing small, and silencing your voice are over. I'm here to affirm that you deserve an amazing life and satisfying relationships. As a wise man once told me, "You can't fight an enemy you don't know exists." Let's have a deeper discussion about how fear can hinder a success-minded woman like you.

Even the most confident woman will have frequent or occasional feelings of vulnerability, insecurity, or fear. These feelings can be stirred up because no one wants to look at their future and imagine spending it alone. So, yes, fear is an understandable gut reaction to uncomfortable situations. It is meant, however, to be a momentary sensation and not the lens through which you view your life. Why? Because God has not given you a spirit of fear!

Fear is also why women tend to settle for less in relationships, at work, and in life. You are capable and equipped to ban fear and scrape those crumbs in the trash. At the end of the chapter, I'll give more specific guidance about how to do this, but first let's look at common clues that you are probably settling for less than you deserve. If you see your situation reflected on this list, don't beat yourself up or judge yourself harshly. I have good news! I believe you are the type of woman who does better once you know better!

Here's what researchers at the *Huffington Post* online say may indicate that you're settling for less than you deserve in your relationships:

> ➤ The relationship brings you down and your significant other doesn't inspire you to do your best.
> ➤ Perhaps he is overly critical or too focused on his needs to be supportive of you.
> ➤ You feel you have to change yourself, your values, goals, or dreams for your partner to accept you.
> ➤ You are in an emotionally or physically abusive relationship. You may have hidden this from family or friends due to shame or co-dependency issues.
> ➤ You usually put your partner's needs before your own.
> ➤ You've been cheated on repeatedly and keep giving him more chances although he has proven to be untrustworthy.
> ➤ You sacrifice too much. You do this because your partner is unable to compromise.
> ➤ You morph into someone else to accommodate his expectations, needs, or desires.
> ➤ You show up for your friends emotionally or for events, but they don't do the same thing for you.
> ➤ You have several clients or co-workers who you're always over-delivering value, and they aren't providing equal value (paying reasonable prices or returning favors).
> ➤ You do favors and exceptional work for your boss, yet you don't receive pay raises or appropriate recognition for what you do.

You might not be in a position where you can clearly see everything that isn't quite right in your relationships and that's okay. Sometimes you just need to ask God to increase your understanding, then expose yourself to educational information that helps raise your awareness levels. When you have become so used to doing things a certain way or after not having healthy boundaries, toxicity can start to feel normal. In contrast, what is actually normal can feel more like a fantasy or something that's out of reach. We'll explore this more deeply in the next chapter. But first, take a deep breath! You can overcome the challenging thoughts you will have to face in order to grow stronger. There's a way to no longer accept crumbs when you deserve the whole cake. Let's identify the trail of crumbs, then sweep them away!

Your Action Plan

Step 1: Identify the problem area.

Where in your life have you been accepting crumbs? This is a good time to seek God through prayer. Is it in your relationships? Is it on your job? Is it concerning your money situation? Maybe you've been accepting crumbs in how you treat yourself. Have you been setting big, bodacious goals? No? Maybe you've been wanting to become physically fit, get healthier, lose weight, or take better care of yourself. In your journal, let's identify those areas and be very specific about how exactly you have been settling for crumbs.

Khandra is a licensed counselor who discovered that she consistently allowed her friendships to drain her energy. She was the "go to" for any friend or family member who needed a quick pep talk, dating advice, or solution to a problem. Essentially, they received free counseling sessions. At first, Khandra felt useful. But over time, she began to feel drained by constantly pouring herself without being filled in return.

So what about you? Have you been taking on relationships where you know they would probably struggle to meet your needs or desires for a healthy relationship?

Think about your finances. Do you find yourself not saving money in a way that makes sense? If so, you're blocking your own wealth building efforts. We'll talk about this in more detail in a later chapter, but for now, write down any problems you're identifying.

Step 2: Pick one area that you want to change.

Once you have trimmed your list down to one area where you want to make a change, congratulations! Now, you get to decide what you really want your life to look and feel like. For this step, limit your vision to the single area you selected for this exercise.

What would you be doing or saying differently if this area of your life was healed? What does it feel like not to settle for crumbs in this area? What emotions do you feel? Who would be there in your ideal scenario? Who would no longer be there in that scenario? Really tap into what it would look and feel like. The better you are able to invoke emotions, the more real your vision will feel.

In your vision, notice your environment. Do you live in a different home? Are you in a different work environment? Do you have a different type of activity that you do with the people that you care about? Paint this picture and don't hold back. Get crazy with it, and it's okay if you aren't completely clear about everything it is that you want. You can always come back and add to what you see. Your only limit is your imagination! Get ready, because in the next step, you'll write this down. Read Step 3 fully before you begin.

Step 3: Write your vision using present tense.

This is easier to do if you actually imagine yourself in the scenario. Notice how it feels to have achieved the vision that you just laid out in the previous step. Let's ask some questions that will help you go deeper and even stir up some of the emotions you will experience when your vision becomes your reality. The more of an emotional connection that you put on that vision that you have for your life, the more likely it is that you will follow through with the plan when opposition appears.

Questions to help you create a clear vision:

> What does it feel like to have/achieve the thing you desire?
> What can you do now that you couldn't do before? How does it feel?
> Are you smiling? Are you alone, with your spouse or with new friends?
> Where are you? What does it look like?
> Is it warm or cool? Are you inside or outdoors?
> What does it feel like to never worry about _____ anymore?
> What do you tell your best friend about how happy you are since you made that one major change?

Sample vision for saving and paying off debt:

"I open my banking app and transfer money to my handful of bills. I feel relieved and relaxed because I'm paying each balance off faster than I expected. I smile as I look at my tithes investment because this is the first year that it feels easy. As I transfer $1,000 to my savings account, I feel so excited I do a little happy dance in my chair because not only are my bills and taxes paid, I'll have $4,500 left over after I buy tickets and hotel for our family vacation to Destin, Florida this year. I'm alone in my home office and admire the beautiful leather furniture and gold-colored decorations I bought with cash I saved. I feel on top of the world since I never have to worry about bill collectors, lack of money, or the stress of late payments ever again. I call my best friend to make plans at the new 5-star restaurant downtown. We can't help but talk and laugh about how good it feels now that both of us are finally getting ahead!"

Step 4: Design an action plan.

You need a written plan of action. It's going to be something that you break down into baby steps so that you know what you have to do in order to achieve the end goal. I don't think goal planning is a one-size-fits-all activity. You have to do a bit of research to find a method that you feel motivated enough to stick with. These basic guidelines will help you focus your prayers and action steps. Sharpen what you create here by getting a copy of a good goal planning book, chart or program. Doing so ensures that you don't end up like most who fail to achieve goals because they haven't even attempted!

Basic Goal Planning Steps:

> Write down your single goal.
> Set a deadline. If you miss it, set another! And another, and another.

List every little step you'll need to make in order to reach the goal. Add more steps as you think of others.

For each step, what obstacles or challenges will you probably encounter? Whose help will you need? What other resources will you require? Be detailed and write it all down. Make your schedule. If you have a 90-day goal, you'll have to plan each month the month before. Each week is planned a week before. Every day is scheduled from the night before.

Choose 3 things you will accomplish every day. Then decide which one is most essential to your achieving your overall goal. That will be the first priority of the day.

Let's say your goal is to take 30 days to establish better boundaries in your relationships.

Your list of priorities might include:

1. Read for 20 minutes every day from a book about boundaries.
2. Write down my boundaries and the consequences for crossing them.
3. Practice "zero tolerance" in enforcing those boundaries each day.

Once you finish the book about boundaries, your new priority might be to read for 20 minutes a day about another topic related to boundaries, like co-dependency, enabling, or effective communication techniques.

Step 5: Implement your plan

Now that you've identified the problem, narrowed it down, visualized your dream life and created a plan, it's time to do the work!

Go Deeper

1. Fear-based thoughts limit your ability to move forward. You will never have use for any thought or habit that tears you down. Read through a few common fear-based thoughts on the list below. In your journal, make a note about any thought that you have struggled with in the recent past. What thoughts can you add to the list? When you're finished, move to the next step.

   ➤ I won't be able to support myself if I give up this job. (self-doubt)
   ➤ No one will accept me because I have children. (disqualifying yourself)
   ➤ This is probably the best that I can do. (limiting beliefs)
   ➤ If I make more money than my family, the people that I care about might feel jealous or they might judge me. (fear of leaving others behind/ rejection)
   ➤ They might think that I'm a snob. (fear of rejection)
   ➤ *I can't do that.* (limiting beliefs)
   ➤ Someday I'll start my business/write a book/ travel. (procrastination, fear of success/failure)
   ➤ They are able to do XYZ because they are rich/ white/male/skinny/famous/a better _____. (making excuses about why YOU can't, but THEY can)
   ➤ *I'll do it later.* (procrastination)

2. Use the **Action Plan** at the end of this chapter to write your vision.

3. **Today, we touch and agree with the following affirmation (read this aloud):**

   "I am a whole woman. Success is my birthright. I am beautifully and perfectly appointed to achieve and have all that the Word of God promises me. I don't take other people's words or actions personally because I know who and Whose I am. In the full power and authority of Jesus, I break any chain or curse that has blinded or crippled me. I do not have a spirit of fear. I have a sound mind and I walk in love according to God's Word. I am the type of woman who does not settle for poor, mediocre, unfair, unkind or unsatisfactory treatment from anyone."

4. Now celebrate! Tell yourself: "I don't settle for crumbs. I am the type of woman who deserves the whole cake!"

"May this be the season your spirit awakens. May this be the season you remember your name. May this be the day your clarity returns."
– Dr. Thema Bryant-Davis

Chapter 5

REBUILDING A SHAKY FOUNDATION

This book has been heavily focused on relationships because women are very relationship orientated. It's in your DNA! I've seen so many women make life decisions in order to please other people (or avoid consequences), which ends up creating bigger problems later. When people make decisions in this manner, it is usually the result of growing up or currently living in a toxic environment. Please note that this chapter will not fully address the toxicity associated with physical, sexual, extreme verbal, financial or emotional abuse. If you are in an abusive environment, please get in front of a professional who specializes in methods for safely exiting volatile situations. Start by Googling a crisis hotline in your city and state.

What exactly do you do when you are in a toxic situation and you're trying to go from 99.9% to a hundred? We'll answer this question and also share tips for negotiating a toxic work environment since most people spend most of their lives at work. There are plenty of women who don't have a plan of action, education or the skill required in order to navigate their situation. If you can relate, then you're not alone.

The first thing you want to do is believe you are a queen, regardless of the environment that you currently may find yourself in. Touch your heart and read that again: *"I am a queen."* Somebody reading this now may doubt my words, so I will tell you a story that will convince you once and for all that your royalty isn't determined by your environment. Your royal calling has been pre-determined by God!

The Jungle Book Story

You may be familiar with the book and movie, *The Jungle Book*. It's about a boy named Mowgli who was rescued and raised by wolves after his family was killed by a tiger. Mowgli grew up in the jungle, hunting and living as an animal. He had those mannerisms and habits because the wolves and other animals told Mowgli he was one of them. Although Mowgli believed he was a wolf, at the end of the day, no human would ever mistake him for a wolf pup! Am I right, or am I right?

So, let's establish that although words have power, "As a man thinketh, so is he." Simply calling a person a name and placing them in an environment doesn't completely alter who they are or cancel their destiny. I'll tell you how to break the grip of false beliefs in a moment, but first I want you to reflect: what names have you been called? What environments have you lived in? Regardless of how toxic the words or environment, it doesn't alter your DNA as a child of The King. Let's go back to our story.

Mowgli eventually moved into the village. There was a time of transition as he adjusted to a new environment, but eventually Mowgli developed the characteristics of other humans in the village. Changing environments and learning new thoughts and behaviors are catalysts for transformation. This next part didn't happen in the story, but imagine what would have happened if Mowgli moved into a house located in the city? What if Mowgli had moved into a luxury home, or even a palace? Let's explore that last idea.

If you put Mowgli in a palace where his parents are the king and queen, he will develop the capabilities, knowledge, opportunities, and bearing of one who is from a royal family. As he is taught about his royal heritage, can you imagine his initial disbelief, awe and eventual acceptance of his new life? There is a process one has to undergo in order to embrace a royal calling. It will take some time because Mowgli came from the jungle! You can't skip the process!

You, dear queen, will have to go through that same process of self-discovery if you have been exposed to toxic environments. In chapter one of this book, I described many of the characteristics of a success-minded woman. You are her. She is you. So, the best thing that you could do in order to accelerate your growth as a success-minded woman is to put yourself in an environment where you're exposed to the skills that success-minded women exemplify every day. You want to put yourself in physical environments where your success mindedness is appreciated and encouraged.

Boundaries

If you currently reside in a "jungle environment," which is when you live with someone who is very critical or unsupportive or even emotionally abusive, you may not have the means (or desire) to just leave. In that situation, you have to create a protective boundary which limits their toxic effect on your emotional and spiritual well-being. When you understand that you are royalty, you have to be clear about the types of behaviors and conversations that you are expecting from the people in your life. These expectations are your standards. Your boundaries are the line you simply will not allow others to cross. If they cross, there are consequences for that. It's your responsibility to make your standards and boundaries known and if someone crosses them, let them know the consequences.

How do you enforce boundaries? You let the people in your life know, "Hey, don't do that. Don't say that. If you do that again, XYZ will happen." Maybe your "XYZ" is if they get loud or disrespectful:

> ➢ You will leave the room
> ➢ You will end the conversation
> ➢ You will pack your bag and move
> ➢ You will withhold something

These are just examples. Whatever the consequence is, you have to make sure that you do not fail to follow through on what you said you would do. As grandmothers everywhere used to say, "People will treat you the way you allow them to treat you." Take time now, to ask yourself: How do I allow others to treat me? How do I want to be treated? How would God want me to be treated? As you answer these questions, be as thorough as possible in coming up with your responses. Your answers are going to guide your actions moving forward.

Two excellent books that expand on this subject are *Boundaries* and *Boundaries in Marriage*, both by Henry McCloud. He is an excellent Christian author and clinical psychologist who gives more specific action steps for how to establish healthy boundaries in your relationships.

Boundaries are present in healthy relationships. You just have to be clear about what your expectations are and also the consequences for violating those boundaries. In chapter four, we already established that queens don't settle for crumbs!

Domestic Abuse and Violence

Even with all the helpful tips in the world about establishing boundaries and being secure in who you are and what you'll expect from another person, it is very challenging to truly flourish in an unhealthy or a toxic environment. Although Mowgli learned to use instinct to survive in certain environments, a child living in the jungle with animals is not ideal. Just like humans weren't designed to be raised by animals, women were not designed to be put down, called names, harmed, abused, manipulated, or controlled in a physical, emotional, or spiritual context. That is not the proper order of things.

If you're finding that, in spite of boundaries, you're still in a situation where you feel like it's affecting your ability to achieve goals, live out your destiny, or follow through with your responsibilities, consider taking things a step further. If physical abuse is involved, please prioritize your safety and find support from a family member or a women's shelter. Connect with a social service provider or agency in order to get more in-depth information about implementing a safety plan. It's outside of the scope of this book to guide you through an abusive situation. Please know that you are on the mind of God. He did not predestine you to live a life where you're consumed with fear, anxiety, or feelings of overwhelm. I want to affirm for you that it is very appropriate to take necessary action for shielding yourself in these situations.

Toxic Work Environments

Many people spend most of their lives working a traditional job. You may not be able to decide who you work with, but you can equip yourself to deal with difficult people in a professional and proactive way. One way to know if your work environment is toxic is to do a self check-up. Do you feel overwhelmed, sad, irritable, or do you have feelings of dread or thoughts like, "I hate my job" or "I hate my boss?" The job search Website, Monster.com offers practical tips for negotiating a workplace that is less than ideal. I've added my own thoughts to their list of suggestions. First, know this: The reactions you have are your body's normal response to stress. "A toxic environment keeps people in a fight-or-flight mindset—the constant pump of cortisol, testosterone, and norepinephrine generates physical, emotional, and mental stress," says Cheri Torres, a leadership coach and author. Here's what you can do to deal with your body's natural response in a healthy way:

1. Have trusted work allies.

Get one or two trusted co-workers that offer a place where you can share your feelings and vent. Just be mindful that you always have to protect yourself by making sure that you never tell your work friends everything. Your off-site network is better suited for discussions about things that could get you reprimanded or fired.

2. Focus on the endgame.

There might be gossip sessions and text threads talking about the evil co-workers, but keep in mind that what you focus on grows. Walk away. Don't participate. Focus on yourself, your goals, your mission, and on staying positive and classy.

3. Be pleasant to everyone.

If you can't be pleasant, at least be neutral. Make a point to stay above the drama. Even when your boss or co-workers are acting up, keep your cool. You will attract who you are, so I'm not suggesting you allow people to get away with poor behavior. If you remain strong, pleasant and professional, others will eventually value you and respond differently, even if it is grudgingly. You'll feel better for not violating your own moral code, too.

4. Balance your work and personal life.

It's not always easy to turn off when your work seems to consume you, but in a toxic environment, you have to prioritize yourself. Boundaries are critical. Establish some things you will not tolerate and stick to them. Some people have made the hard decision to turn off their phone after a certain hour or ignore messages from co-workers. Others refuse to take work home. Your to-do list will always have something on it, but for your own sanity, it is healthy to establish a close of business hour. If you work from home or are a stay-at-home mom, it is still important to establish a time when all work must cease and rest begins.

5. Be open to another opportunity.

Whatever you are facing on your job doesn't have to be a permanent situation. You always have options. If that means you spend time every day developing a skill set that allows you to leave your job for a better opportunity; plan for it! If you know you are working towards a brighter future, it is certainly easier to endure painful seasons.

Go Deeper

1. What parts of Mowgli's story can you relate to? What is one thing you are willing to do today to help you remember how God defines you?

2. Pray right now and ask God to reveal the people and resources that can help you get exposure to fresh and new environments and opportunities. After you pray, start searching social media for groups and pages for women in business, women writers, Christian moms, women in engineering… Search topics that interest you. Join groups, participate and connect with others who are doing the things you want to do.

3. Do you need additional support in breaking free from an abusive environment? Visit https://www. thehotline.org. If your Internet usage is being monitored, it is better to call the National Domestic Violence Hotline at 800-799-7233.

"Your strength doesn't come from winning. It comes from struggles and hardship. Everything that you go through prepares you for the next level."

— Germany Kent

Chapter 6

YOUR NEXT LEVEL

You're ready to go to the next level in your life and I'm proud of you. I'm not saying implementing any of this will be easy, but it will be worth it. I've created a list of concepts that I want you to start thinking, dreaming, and praying about. You will be amazed at how God will give you revelation and opportunities once you start talking with Him about these areas of your life. Let's start with one of the most important areas of focus.

Belief

The first step to up leveling your life, relationships and money situation is believing you can. I recently watched a TEDx Talk where a psychologist did an experiment that proved people could make themselves lose weight if participants simply believed the information they watched in the training video. The interesting thing about these experiments was that the results of the blood tests taken before and after participants watched the video revealed that the brain released fat-inhibiting hormones in response to what they learned. Their brain released hormones simply because *they believed*.

Can you see the power of belief? This experiment is one of many that proves our thoughts definitely have a positive or negative impact on our bodies and lives. Allow me to be the trusted authority figure in your life who provides you with the training and information that will help you up level. Believe in your ability to change for the better. " For as he thinketh in his heart, so is he" (Proverbs 23:7).

Call on the promises of God and if you don't know them already, make a point to learn them. Review the chapter on mindset and revisit the exercise at the end. But whatever you do, no longer underestimate the role your powerful mind and imagination have in shaping your future.

Discipline

There is a saying, "How you do one thing is how you do everything." The ability to outperform yourself is hard work and requires a strong, disciplined mind and behaviors. Instead of trying to add discipline exclusively in the area where you want to see the greatest improvement, look to be disciplined in everything you do. Establish a minimum standard or code that you refuse to slip beneath. As you look at the different areas of your life, where can you add a stroke of discipline?

In my own life, sometimes I am tempted to sleep in or cut corners. It is tempting to make excuses like "I deserve a break." At the time, it seems legitimate. The Bible instructs us "...to love discipline; it is stupid to hate correction" (Proverbs 12:1 NLT). I have to be intentional about what I do, and I make sure to have brothers in my life to help with accountability. I want to move forward in my life, so I must meet my own minimum standards.

Here are a few areas that call for discipline in the lives of most people:

> - Duration and frequency of exercise
> - Portions and types of food you eat
> - Amount of alcohol purchased and used
> - Enforcing or creating a financial budget
> - Frequency of prayer and meditation
> - Regular church attendance and active participation
> - Types of shows and movies watched
> - Level of cleanliness in and outside of the home
> - Social media consumption
> - How you talk to and interact with others
> - Quality of time spent doing productive activities

What can you add to this list?

Habits

Be willing to admit that one of the reasons you probably don't already have what you desire is you aren't currently doing enough of the things needed to push yourself forward. A lot of these things consist of daily habits. Daily habits are the steps you take each day, rain or shine, in good times or bad moods. Habits go hand-in-hand with discipline.

CiCi is an entrepreneur whose daily habits include waking up at 5:30 a.m. Monday through Saturday. She gets up at 7 a.m. on Sundays. She spends time in prayer and meditation before writing her goals and affirmations for the day. She makes her bed, goes for a 3-mile walk, showers, then enjoys breakfast while she listens to a motivational YouTube video or podcast. She accomplishes this all before 9 a.m., which is when she sits at her desk to reach out to potential clients. CiCi plans her clothing, meals, goals, and motivational videos the night before she needs them. She also makes sure her Bible, notebook, pen and water bottle are next to the bed so that she doesn't waste time getting organized in the morning. Preparation has helped CiCi establish daily habits that keep her focused on her desired outcome.

Ask yourself these hard questions:

> ➢ What daily habits do I currently have?
> ➢ How do these habits help me?
> ➢ Which habits waste my time, money or slow my growth?
> ➢ Do I know what things I need to do each day in order to organize or simplify my life?
> ➢ Am I willing to do things other people won't do?

> ➤ Am I willing to wake up earlier, or give up sleep time?
> ➤ Am I willing to save money for additional training, business conferences or airfare?
> ➤ Am I willing to "put myself out there" to meet new people?
> ➤ Am I willing to change my diet or exercise habits?
> ➤ Am I willing to get rid of_____ (fill in the blank with your most uncomfortable habit)?

Your Physical Body

This isn't about being thin, curvy or sexually attractive. This is about honestly assessing whether your physical health, appearance, and conditioning allow you to freely be, do, and have everything God promises. Do you have the energy you need to get up earlier so that you can meditate and spend quality time with God? If you want to be a well-known businessperson, motivational speaker, an in-demand author, professor, or other professional, will your current physical state hinder you from showing up as your best self?

Thirty years ago, I used to dream of ministering to a church filled with people who were hungry for the word of God. Today, I'm an apostle over seven churches and also serve as Second Presiding Bishop of the Full Gospel Baptist Church Fellowship. There is always a meeting, conference call, or line of people looking to me for leadership and counsel. I'm constantly casting the vision, putting out fires, delegating, and negotiating. I also have a wife, five children and three grandchildren. As an in-demand bishop, it sometimes feels like I live in the airport. But despite my schedule, I make time to exercise and eat as healthy as I can. I'm not perfect, but I clearly understand that if I neglect myself, my energy decreases, stress increases, and I begin to pour from an empty cup.

My wife also serves as a fine example of what a woman can achieve personally and professionally when you make health a priority. Lady Brister has been a committed health advocate who has taught our children to be physically active and she has maintained the energy required to keep up with everything our life demands of us.

I also had the privilege of growing up in a home where my mother was very health conscious. She lived for almost 94 years and I believe that is attributed to her decision to never touch alcohol, tobacco or drugs.

I'm teaching you something I live and know firsthand. I strongly advise you to adjust your nutrition, medications, exercise routine, clothing choices, make up application, or whatever it might be, so that you are physically able to grasp, hold on to, and survive whatever the next level requires of you. One day you will thank me for this advice!

Goal Setting

In an earlier chapter, we briefly explored how to set goals. It's worth bringing up this topic again because most people are trapped in a cycle of doing just enough to get by. Before you start to wonder if you are doing enough, please understand this: Your identity is not defined by what you do or don't do. You are already enough. Although, I'm trying to help you realize that you are already enough, you still need a way to measure whether or not you are using your time in the most productive ways.

Setting and achieving goals will help you know the answer to this question, "Am I doing enough?" If you didn't do the goal setting exercise in chapter three, please go back now and follow the instructions. While reading is important to growth, I also want you to implement what you learn and finish what you start. This habit pushes you forward in life and builds your confidence as a woman. So, practice goal setting and try different methods until you discover the one or two that help you stay accountable to yourself.

Multiple Streams of Income

Whether you are comfortable with the idea or not, these days, you are a wise woman if you have a few different ways to make money. It's a rare man who wants to find a good woman who can stay home with the kids while he goes and earns the money. Also gone are the days when a good education results in a job where you can expect to earn a high salary, advance with the company, and eventually retire and earn a pension. I support higher learning, but at the same time, I also understand the game. And the outcome of the college and student loan game usually results in more debt than the student can easily manage over a lifetime.

I can go on and on about the financial times, but I want you to understand one key thing. It isn't all doom and gloom. In a 2018 article I found online, *Forbes* states that women, and specifically African American women, are among the top demographics for new startup companies in the United States today. The article goes on to say that although Black women lack the resources available to other racial groups, they continue to soar. I definitely support women who choose to get serious about network marketing companies, online boutiques, and digital product sales. I appreciate others who become lash and nail technicians, realtors, motivational speakers, authors, and other service providers. I also want to encourage you to dream bigger.

Women are now opening construction companies, engineering firms, global makeup, clothing, and product lines, as well as technology startups. Women are securing multi-million dollar government contracts, and even getting priority during the bidding process. You know what else women are doing? Women are leveraging the online world to sell products and services to the global community. They are using their own Websites, social media, and giant platforms like Amazon.com to do it.

Why shouldn't you get in on the action? I'm not telling you to quit your job today and go start a side hustle! I am saying that we are living in a time where you have to be able to look out for yourself. One way to do that is to create additional ways to make money. If your job goes away, or if you decide to give homeschooling, world travel, or missions trips a try, you will have the financial flexibility to do so.

Jessica owns an online boutique. Stocking her store and servicing her customers is a full-time job. She makes money in different ways and she got really good at what she does. People wanted to learn from her, so she started coaching clients about how to open their own boutiques. It was difficult keeping up with so many individuals, so she began a group coaching program she taught once a week. She decided to record her teachings and compile them to sell as a course. She then charged a much higher price for individual coaching and referred those who couldn't afford it to her online course. She then wrote a book about opening a boutique. After the book, her social media following really grew, so she began offering a monthly membership. Members would pay a monthly fee in order to be a part of her "tribe" of entrepreneurial women. She then began selling a resource list, checklists, and another book. She also began to travel and speak to women's groups.

Everywhere Jessica went, she promoted her social media accounts and her following grew. In addition, she began to participate in affiliate marketing programs with other companies. These companies would pay Jessica to tell her social media followers about products and services she was already using in her business. Let's count up Jessica's income streams that resulted from ONE business:

1. Retail sales from an online boutique
2. Individual coaching
3. Group coaching
4. Online course sales
5. Book sales
6. Monthly membership subscriptions
7. Digital resource list
8. Speaking opportunities
9. Affiliate marketing

Jessica's goal is to build a business where there are many passive income streams. This means that she does the work one time yet continues to get paid over and over again. What ideas does this stir up for you? Write down your ideas. Now let's talk about how to have a money strategy.

Money Strategy

There are a lot of really good books about how to effectively budget and save your money. Everything you need to know is already out there, you just need to become a student. I'm not going to spend a lot of time discussing budgets and retirement accounts, but I want you to understand some basic concepts you can research further.

A money strategy is a plan for how to get profitable and grow your investments. To do this you will use tactics, which break down how to reach your money goals. Essentially, instead of you making decisions based on which bills are due, you take charge of your money and tell each dollar what to do. Let's go back to Jessica's story. She has multiple ways to make money, but needs a plan for how to increase the income and accomplish her goals of saving enough money to invest in multiple real estate properties. This is where it pays to develop the habit of having a vision and writing goals.

One simple strategy for raising funds quickly is to earn as much money as possible, while spending as little as possible. Jessica might decide to reduce or eliminate as much debt as possible. She could quickly reduce the amount of money she spends on bills by moving in with her parents to save on rent or find a smaller apartment to lease. She could trade her car in. She could shop at secondhand clothing stores or stop shopping for clothes, period. What other ways can you think of to lower your bills? There are many ways to reduce spending, but each requires discipline. Thankfully, you were built to accomplish hard things. It's in your DNA.

At the same time that Jessica is reducing expenses, she needs to increase her income. She is already a busy entrepreneur so doesn't want too many demands on her time. She could create more books, e-books, and courses to sell. Here are some other ideas if writing isn't your thing.

You could also, rent out a portion of your home on a short-term rental site like Airbnb.com. Google that idea. You could also put bunk beds in a spare bedroom and offer overnight care for children. This could be a dream solution for parents who work nights or just want a date night option. Get creative! I once read a news story about a college student who lived in a state that didn't have Krispy Kreme donuts. He began hauling donuts across the state line and sold them for double what he paid for them. What about you? How could you get creative using the Facebook Marketplace, Amazon. com, Etsy.com, eBay.com, or by going door-to-door? Give the questions throughout this chapter deeper thought. Your money solution is near!

Allow yourself to dream and expose yourself to people and ideas that intimidate you. No longer will you critique or judge people who are doing more than you. Instead, let their innovations and successes drive you. There is enough pie for everyone. You are the type of woman who is bold enough to get yourself a slice or two.

Go Deeper

1. Ultimately, if you truly desire to up level your life and money situation, you have to answer these two questions honestly: Do I really want it? How bad?

2. What is the first area you will focus on in order to up level your life: money or business? What is your first step in graduating from an idea to a plan? Write it down. Commit to do the work. Commit to never going backwards.

3. Find a book about money management and order a copy today. I recommend getting a highlighter, pen, and notebook so that you can reinforce your learning. I believe in your ability to tell your dollars how to behave! Walk confidently in that today.

4. For the next 6 months, commit to retraining your brain with thoughts and behaviors that encourage positive beliefs, habits, and discipline. Unfollow every Facebook and Instagram celebrity and entertainer who are just there for entertainment. Right now, they are a distraction from your re-training. Spend 10 minutes a day, replacing all of their pages with pages from businesswomen, entrepreneurs, positive quote pages, and inspirational people. Only spend 10 minutes on this! The rest of the day, you'll be busy implementing the plans you listed in #2.

"The best love is the
kind that awakens the soul,
that makes us reach for
more, that plants the fire
in our hearts and brings
peace to our minds. That's
what I hope to give
you forever."
- The Notebook

Chapter 7

"WIFE MATERIAL"

The traits that are already within you are the single most important factor in determining the quality of mate you attract. I have good news! God has created you with infinite potential. That means there are no limits to what you can do or develop within yourself. As discussed earlier in this book, you have access to everything you need to be a whole woman. All you need is a desire, belief, and a willingness to take the appropriate action.

Have you already made a list of attributes you would like your future mate to have? Take that same list and evaluate how much of yourself you have devoted to developing those same qualities. If you are a woman who describes yourself as "the ideal mate" and "wife material," how have you put that belief to the test? You aren't wife material simply because you think you are. You are wife material because you actually have the qualities that increase the likelihood of attracting the type of husband you prayed about. I created a list of traits that, as you develop them within yourself, will reduce the likelihood of attracting the type of man who isn't for you. I don't think you'll meet too many (if any!) men who actually sit around with a "wife checklist." He's not reading through a pile of notes in order to decide whether a woman will be the type to build him up and hold him down when he needs it most. He's more likely to base his decision to marry on where he is financially, his career, and a deep emotional connection with a woman. There comes a time when a man begins to reflect on his life. If he is in a relationship, friends and family might start to apply some pressure about when he will settle down. Only then does he begin to imagine his life with or without the woman he loves. As you can see, the process a man goes through when choosing a life partner is different from how you pick a mate.

Let's talk through a few of the traits that help ensure you are truly unforgettable when your man begins to imagine a future with or without you. However, the following information is not intended to be used to manipulate men or misrepresent yourself. Use it to be even more clear about who you are as a whole woman!

Traits of an Unforgettable Woman

- ➢ Godliness
- ➢ Loyalty
- ➢ Hardworking
- ➢ Rarely complains or nags
- ➢ Kindness
- ➢ Patience
- ➢ Attentiveness
- ➢ Doesn't seek to change his personality/masculine traits
- ➢ Willingness to please self and him
- ➢ Respectfulness
- ➢ Reliability
- ➢ Improves self
- ➢ Joy
- ➢ Open and honest communication
- ➢ Embraces her sexuality and femininity

As a godly woman, you try to honor the Lord with your life, so you are honest, forgiving, and won't seek out a lifestyle that would offend God. Being godly is a wonderful trait to possess because it covers a lot! However, don't mistake godliness for perfection. A godly woman is a praying woman. As such, you exercise grace and guard your tongue by being tactful. As a godly woman, wisdom is your teacher because a man isn't usually looking to hear every deep thought that comes to mind. You want to know when to press, how to pray and in what way you can bless those around you.

Also, be honest with yourself. If you have a problem or concern, pray about it, come up with possible solutions and then express your truth in a respectable manner. Honesty will let your yes mean yes and your no mean no. Don't leave it to your partner to figure out whether you were actually hungry when you said you weren't. Or that you meant no when you said, "Fine with me." You will demonstrate your ability to be consistent with the truth every single time you deliver on your promises.

With regard to loyalty, most people probably define that as someone who doesn't have sex or intimate bonds with other people outside of the relationship. It's that, but it's also so much more. When you are loyal, you put others before yourself and stick by their side in good times and during the bad. It's about how you show up in the relationship when the money gets tight, or when the overtime at work or school kicks in. It's about what you do when an extended illness or a major disagreement happens. How does the relationship suffer when you don't feel supported or you feel overwhelmed by work, kids, and other responsibilities? Are you able to show the same level of support, friendship and attentiveness during the hard times? A loyal woman can and will. Please note: this discussion does not apply to toxic or abusive relationships.

A hardworking woman contributes. You can choose to be a woman who is capable of starting a business and family. Your ideal mate will value a true partner who will put effort into creating, sustaining and growing what they build together. Doing hard work doesn't mean doing all the work. It means that you have tenacity, grit and the desire to finish what you start. It is important to not be a quitter when it comes to relationships. Hard times call for couples to pull together and put in the hard work together.

There isn't a really tactful way to write this next part, but many women have a hard time accepting that complaining, having an argumentative nature, and asking for the same thing more than twice (a.k.a. nagging) truly grieves a man's soul. (See Proverbs 19:13; 21:9; 21:19; 25:24; and 27:15) Complaining is when a person constantly expresses their annoyance or dissatisfaction. Since this is such a common characteristic, let's spend some time unpacking how a person can get to a place where they complain all the time.

Two of the traits that create a complaining spirit are a negative mindset and ungratefulness. Don't be too hard on yourself if you struggle with this because being positive and grateful do not come naturally to a lot of people, so you're not alone. A lot of you have been through multiple heartaches, mistreatment and pain and you haven't healed from it yet. When life has hit you with a lot, you start to anticipate the blows by bracing yourself even in situations that aren't meant to cause pain.

You might develop a defensive posture that looks something like this: A man walks up, smiles and says hello. Instead of smiling back, you give a side-eye and say, "What? No, I'm not interested and no, you can't have my number!" Yet, you have been praying that you'll meet a nice man! Listen to your mentor on this one: even if you weren't attracted to the man, in most scenarios, there isn't a good reason to be negative towards someone who says, "Hello."

If your pain was caused within relationships, you can slowly develop a negative mindset and not even know it is happening. You may start to think the worst in order to avoid disappointment. *I'll hurt you before you can hurt me* is a common unconscious thought process that causes women to sabotage themselves, relationships and opportunities. You don't have to trace the root of complaints back to childhood or anything. Just know that actively complaining tears down others and unnecessarily makes everything feel worse.

There was a season in my own life where I didn't know I had started to become negative and ungrateful. One day, I caught myself in the act of complaining. I was driving home after a long and stress-filled day. In the car, I remember thinking I had accomplished a lot that day, but I felt drained. I was looking forward to coming home to my sanctuary and turning off my brain. I'm sure many of you reading this have felt the same way. Unfortunately, I approached things the wrong way. I remember walking in the door and the environment just felt out-of-control. The kids were everywhere and so were their toys. I'm not proud to say that I began to complain about the noise and mess. I was just getting warmed up for more complaints when I caught my wife's eye. I could see that she was exhausted too. I closed my mouth, bent down and started picking up toys. In that moment, I was filled with regret and realized that complaining can ruin a relationship. It only makes everyone feel more stressed, negative, and worn down. When you complain, you're just tempting your partner to start finding even worse faults in you!

When you are kind, attentive, and joyful, you are a welcomed addition to any gathering. People are attracted to those who usually smile, are generous and who have a positive attitude about life. As a kind woman you "speak life", consider others' feelings, and seek to brighten the lives of those around you. If you are considerate of other people, you are probably patient too. Patience is an important trait because when you keep bumping up against the many differences between a man and woman, you have to choose to face conflicts with grace.

You will know the value of patience and kindness when there are children pulling you in different directions, even while bills, meals, chores, extended family, and your career all have their hands out, too. Even with the most supportive husband on the planet, that scenario can wear down even the 100% woman. But it's real life. So kindness clearly doesn't mean weakness. As a matter of fact, it takes strength to give of yourself when you'd rather be by yourself. It doesn't cost anything to display kindness, but it is a priceless trait to possess.

It is very common for both men and women to try to change their partners. However, learn about the distinctively male traits so that you are less likely to try changing those things that are a part of his DNA. His desire to pursue, conquer, compete, protect, relax, communicate differently, think differently, and view the world differently are not things to "fix." These masculine traits are how God created a man. Understanding this will save you a lifetime of frustrations!

Have you ever met a woman who got involved with a man then put her own goals, dreams, ideas and interests on hold while she adopted his priorities? He may have even encouraged her to make his interests her only priority because many men enjoy being the center of his woman's world. My advice? Just because he likes it, doesn't mean you should go along with it! You have to stay focused and strong. In a dating scenario, if a man is not your husband, he does not come first, period! He may also lack awareness of how important it is for you both to fulfill your life purpose. It takes strength to maintain your identity, relationships and interests that please you. In the long run, he will respect you more when you keep your priorities in order. If you are not married, those priorities are God, yourself, your children, career and then him.

What does it mean to be a respectful woman? You'll know you are being a respectful woman by your actions. It's something you do. For example, you'll guard your tongue by not saying things that put down, emasculate, or insult his strengths, thoughts, abilities or potential. In contrast, respect is something that happens in your heart and mind. It's when you deeply admire his qualities, abilities and achievements. It is an *earned* benefit for a man who demonstrates consistent leadership, prioritizes your heart, and makes his intentions clear. As such, respect is not freely given.

A man also likes a reliable woman he can count on. He should generally see that you are consistent with your boundaries, behavior, and emotional state. This doesn't mean you stop speaking your mind, nor does he have unlimited access to your time and attention. Actually, maintaining a level of mystery during the dating process is a good thing (see chapter eight, Strategic Dating). However, you should try to be consistent with your boundaries, behavior and emotional state.

Carissa's Story – Maintaining Her Own Interests

Carissa was a busy professional who also had a group of active friends that she would do girl trips, brunch dates and other activities with. She served on a ministry at church and was also thinking about going back to college to earn a certificate that would help towards her next promotion. When she started getting serious about Darren, she made sure he knew that her friendships and activities were an important part of her life. She was excited about them growing together, but she wasn't afraid to tell Darren, "Not tonight, but we can meet Thursday."

She actively kept her commitments to herself or with her friends. Darren respected her hustle and secretly liked that she was different from other women he dated who were always available whenever he texted, called, or wanted to see them. Carissa liked having personal goals and other friendships that occupied her thoughts, which protected her from getting carried away by her feelings for Darren. In past relationships, she had rushed into things and ignored red flags partly because she didn't maintain outside interests and priorities.

***

What does it mean to improve yourself? It means that you do what you can to be the best version of yourself. The only man that doesn't appreciate your desire for self-improvement is an insecure man. All people have insecurities at times, but a man who is insecure at his core will try to pull you down in order to feel better. Avoid him! (See chapter three for ways to improve yourself.)

You are a joyful woman when you have a positive "we got this!" attitude regardless of the circumstance. When you are full of joy, you are also thankful and grateful. "Rejoice always, pray continually, give thanks in all circumstances; for this is God's will for you in Christ Jesus." (1 Thessalonians 5:16-17) If you are thankful, praying and grateful, it is impossible to have a posture that would be described as a "bad attitude." At the root of a bad attitude is a woman who either does not know her attitude is awful, doesn't care that it's awful, or has walls up to protect herself from being hurt. You have power in your tongue right now to pluck out any root of offense, bitterness, unresolved hurt, trauma or pain, unforgiveness, resentment, mistrust, or pride. Cast off anything that would keep you from being a cheerful, happy, joy-filled, grateful, thankful woman who is also a light that draws others. Involve a counselor in your life who can point out the attitudes, beliefs and patterns that hinder your growth.

Another ideal trait you, as a good woman, will possess is open and honest communication. This means you tell the truth about circumstances and how you feel. You don't try to get your man to "read your mind," or "just know" your thoughts, feelings, or intentions. In order to have open and honest communication, you have to also learn how to listen well and be aware of your own deeper, more vulnerable feelings. At the same time, communication isn't a one-way street. Pick a mate who doesn't "punish" you with a toxic response when you respectfully express your thoughts or feelings. Healthy communication patterns are a critical foundational piece for marriage, parenting, your career, and long-term friendships. Learn to listen well and develop your ability to "hear" the emotional root of what your partner is saying. This is an advanced skill that you won't just know! Many of us have not had truly healthy communication patterns modeled in our early relationships. As with many of the topics I discuss throughout this book, you must study to show yourself approved.

Another trait that men value in a woman is how well you embrace your sexuality and femininity. Show appreciation when a man opens the door and caters to you. Have a hint of flirtation and allure. This isn't something that is openly sexual, seductive or provocative. You can let him know that you are interested and attracted to him every time you laugh at his jokes and look at him with admiration in your eyes. There are things that you can do that are distinctly feminine and attractive: Tastefully styling your hair, applying a natural makeup, keeping skin soft and clean, having a fresh, sweet scent, and caring for hands, feet, and nails. A man still wants a woman who is comfortable allowing him to be "the man." Again, this directs us back to an earlier point: if you understand masculine tendencies, you won't get stuck in the frustrating cycle of trying to change traits that God built into his DNA.

Your Best Trait

The best thing you can do for attracting the man of your prayers is being as close to whole as possible. You don't have to have it all together, but you can teach yourself how to rely on God to aid you in becoming the best version of yourself.

Go Deeper

1. Write down the traits you're looking for in a husband. On a separate sheet, use a scale of 1-10 to evaluate how much of each trait you currently have. Then ask a trusted friend to rate you. Compare notes. What areas do you need to build up? What book or resource can you start reading in order to build yourself in one area? Write it here.

2. When you feel upset about something someone is saying, it is a clue that there is a triggered area within yourself. Was there something that you read that gave you a stronger emotional response than other sections of the chapter? Analyze why you felt strongly about what you read. Can you come up with two other explanations about why you felt upset, outraged, or defensive? As your mentor, I want you to challenge your beliefs so that you can move towards wholeness.

3. If you desire a bigger dose of any of the traits I wrote about in this chapter, the more you practice them, the more they will become a part of your DNA. So, practice with your friends, family and every stranger you meet. Deepen your compassion by praying for your pastor, neighbor or stranger until you feel it in your soul. Some of these traits just require you to start being aware of, and caring more deeply about, other people's perspectives and how your words and actions make them feel. You must be willing to look outside of your own thoughts and feelings in order to connect with others in a new way. Don't dismiss this, try it!

"No matter how love-sick a woman is, she shouldn't take the first pill that comes along."
- Joyce Brothers

Chapter 8

THE DATING MINDSET

This topic rightfully deserves its own book and there are at least 100,000 titles available on the topic of dating and relationships. Yet and still, with all of the information available, many of you are not experiencing the results you desire. There is a dating mindset that you want to have in order to bump into less heartbreak and disappointments. If you approach each date with thoughts of, *I hope this one works out* or fantasies of *he could be the one*, you put yourself at a disadvantage. Guys can sense when you are overly impressed, eager-to-please or naïve. If you are hoping he could be "the one" and you have only known each other a few weeks, you can unknowingly come across as clingy or desperate. This puts you in a position to settle for crumbs. See chapter four, "You Don't Settle for Crumbs," for insight into how unhealed wounds create fear and desperation.

As your mentor, I have encouraged you throughout this book to be open to seeking the support and assessment of a mental health professional for an objective insight into your relationship patterns and habits. If you have ever been abandoned, abused, divorced, or a victim of low self-esteem, these deeper insights could give you a real edge over the men who desire to manipulate or use you. Once you are aware of the cycles, you can protect your weak spots while you heal. As a single person, you deserve to approach this season with a spirit of curiosity, fun and adventure. This is possible, with the right dating mindset.

Let's be clear: when you develop a dating mindset, it takes a minute to work. It requires much effort and at times, you will be tempted to undo all your work. So, don't just adopt the mindsets and behaviors that feel comfortable or make you feel less lonely. Queen, you are the most valuable commodity on the planet, and you should never forget it again! So, are you ready to learn a dating mindset that will help improve your dating skills? I see you out there nodding, "Yes, yes, yes!"

Dating Mindset #1: You are the prize.

I've been trying to teach you this on every page of this book! It is the mindset you have to take on if you want to date a variety of desirable men. When you meet a man who does not understand that you are the prize or if he doesn't agree, move on. This needs to be your posture, period! A lot of men have grown up not valuing women. A lot of women have grown up not knowing their value and not valuing themselves. The good news is God defines you. Not your mama, daddy, or last "no good" boyfriend. You aren't spoiled or arrogant. You are wife material, queen material, and the Bomb-dot-com. You are the prize! As you meet men and decide whether you want to get to know them further, continue to remind yourself of who you are and Whose you are as a child of God!

Dating Mindset #2: Go slow in order to get to know him.

Some of you act like dating is a race. When the physical or emotional intensity between you builds quickly, you will unknowingly either push quality men away or miss the red flags from men who are trying to play games with you. Anybody can do and say right things for a month. So, you can't be out here "catching feelings," becoming exclusive, and thinking about a long-term relationship after a week of his daily texts and phone calls.

Build the relationship at the same time that you're developing an actual friendship. This goal will help you build a healthy foundation for your future. If you want a quality relationship that lasts, stop taking on "wife duties" before you've established a solid friendship. How long does it take to know you have a loyal friend? Four months? Six months? 12 months? Are you going to open your entire body, life, money, heart, home, and mind to a person you knew for a short time? At the time that I'm writing this in Spring 2020, the world is going through a pandemic and most people live under quarantine right now. This is not the time to fall in love with a man who hasn't done anything more than text or talk to you by phone.

Tisha's Story: Too Fast Too Soon

Tisha met Terrell online using Facebook's new dating feature. Terrell lived in her city and he called her every morning and liked to Facetime with her before bed. He was so consistent with his attention, often texting just to say, "Hey" during the day. Sometimes they talked for hours. When they met for their first date, the two hung out for hours just laughing and talking about any and everything. He really seemed to know her and was so attentive.

Tisha knew Terrell had all the traits she desired in a man. He made a high salary, said he loved God, looked good, and was considerate. He even ordered food to her at work when she told him she had to work late and paid for all of their dates. He told her about his ex-wife and how she abandoned him and his daughters, leaving him a single father. He said his divorce would be finalized in three months, and it was overwhelming at times. He told her how hard it is for him to trust people.

Tisha felt overwhelmed too... overwhelmed with compassion. She couldn't believe someone would abandon such a kind, strong, good man. She put her arms around Terrell and vowed to herself that she would never hurt him, too. In a week, he asked to be exclusive. She eagerly said, "YES!" Later that night, Tisha had the best sex she ever had. Terrell then invited Tisha to meet his family. They loved her! His mom snapped some pics of the happy couple and posted them to Facebook. That day, Terrell said, "By this time next year, I would love to make you my wife."

Tisha thanked God for finally answering her prayers. She was going to have a husband!

But Tisha has only known Terrell for 2 weeks. In reality, the two are still strangers. If Tisha discovers red flags in another 2 weeks or 2 months, she'll be very likely to justify or ignore them. At that point, she will be so deeply attached to him and the fantasy future she imagined, that it will be very hard to emotionally untangle herself. Moving too fast is one sure way to trap yourself.

When you are meeting people, stop looking for a reason to fall in love! Instead, look for the qualities you want in a husband. You need to give yourself an opportunity to observe and check for consistency. Anybody can be on their best behavior for a month or two! Also, believe me when I tell you, a man will never value a prize that he obtains with little effort. Read it again. I don't care what modern day folks try to tell you! If you are having sex or telling your entire life story during the first 7 days of meeting a man, there is a 99% chance that he will not seriously consider you for marriage. In a man's mind, the most valued prizes do not come quickly or with ease. As a woman, you need him to develop an emotional connection to you. He has to invest time and effort into getting to know you in order for that to happen. Period! In order to slow things down long enough for you to assess his real intentions and establish a friendship:

- ➤ Keep dates under 3 hours. This will build his anticipation for "next time."
- ➤ Act interested, but don't always be so accessible and available when he texts, calls or wants to see you.
- ➤ Let him show you, not tell you who he is. Be cautious and alert until you have a ring, wedding date, deposit down on the venue, and the pastor is on the way!

> ➢ Once you have sex, you take away his incentive to pursue. Read that again!

Dating Mindset #3: Don't talk too much.

When you're doing all the talking, you are giving details about who you are while missing important insights into his personality, character, and intentions. A better strategy is to ask questions. It shouldn't feel like an interrogation or job interview, but make no mistake: you are interviewing him for the most prized position on the planet! In order to make the right decision, you have to listen for what he isn't saying. This is a skill you may need to study and develop.

What does this look like? If you ask a direct question but don't receive direct answers in response, what is he really saying to you by not answering the question? Many women have allowed men to talk their way into a relationship or "situationship" although the man wasn't offering anything of value except words. He knew what you wanted to hear because you told him everything he needed to know in order to present himself in a way that appealed to you. He also learns about your deeper thoughts and motivations by watching your social media pages. Be careful about the clues you leave for potential mates.

I have respect for my brothers who are not trying to manipulate or harm women. However, there are men who are scrolling your social media page and texting "what are you looking for in a man/relationship?" because they want to snatch your soul. A lot of women will do the most for a man who spends money on her and knows how to say the right things. It benefits you to talk less, ask questions, and listen more. Avoid attaching yourself to anyone who doesn't want to answer your questions and who can't, or won't, effectively

17

communicate. Here are a few tips for communicating more strategically:

> Avoid posting on your social media accounts that you are upset, lonely or sad. Stop giving random men too much insight into what makes your heart beat faster. He needs to work and put effort into getting to know you in order to value you. Men like to work for the prize.

> Be careful when a man asks you questions like the following: "What are you looking for in a man? What do you want from me? What are you looking for in a relationship? Why did you and your last man break up? What is the most romantic thing anyone has ever done for you? What was your last man like?" Answer with information that lets you see how he interprets things. For example, answer the question, "What are you looking for in a man?" by saying, "I like a strong, reliable man." Don't give him specific examples of what he can do to demonstrate that he is strong or reliable. Let him show you who he is inside, not show you who you told him you want him to be!

Dating Mindset #4: Don't chase love.

A man values a woman who presents a challenge. Don't interpret "challenge" to mean "difficult." A woman pursues a man by texting and calling all the time, planning the dates, driving to see him, buying gifts, running errands, taking on wife duties, watching his kids, or making it clear that she's always available. Your pursuit does not create an environment for him to connect emotionally. Many women mistakenly believe, "The more I do, the more he will value me." Actually, the more you do that is above what he is currently doing for you, the more he will relax and allow you to take the lead. Men are just wired this way.

This doesn't mean that all men are trying to run game. It means that men will take the most direct and logical way to achieving a goal. For example, if you make it clear through your body language and conversation that you are already sexually open and hanging on his every word, he is assured that he doesn't have to exert more energy in order to win you. Remember, it is you who sets the standard, pace, and tone for the relationship. If he is interested in you and you wait for him to text, call, plan, compliment and buy gifts first, he will do it. What I'm writing isn't an insult to men at all, because we are God's design and He doesn't make mistakes!

- ➤ For every three texts he initiates, you initiate one text. This isn't a ratio you have to stick to "or else." Just use wisdom. Whatever you do, avoid having a desperate or needy vibe.
- ➤ Let him buy you gifts first. When you do buy him a gift, don't let the value or thought behind your gift be more than what he has given you. Match his energy.
- ➤ Let him plan dates although you should offer to pay your share. Don't act entitled. He doesn't owe you a meal, ladies. This is a new day and age. When you offer to cover your meal, you come across as financially independent, not needy. He can never think you owe him something later. Let him pay if he insists.
- ➤ If he doesn't make efforts to consistently meet with you in person, he is likely focused on work, not highly interested in you, or he is exploring other female options. A man will pursue a woman he desires.

Dating Mindset #5: Learn to spot "game."

Men are really good at studying women and many have become good at manipulating you in order to get "wife favors" without the commitment. Here are some common games men play:

> They text you a lot, then pull back their attention. This usually causes women to begin pursuing the man as they try to figure out, "What's wrong? What did I do? Are you okay? What happened?" Never get too attached to his constant texting and attention, so if he pulls back, it will not faze you.

> They text you "GM," "wyd," "hey," "GN," and other one word replies without really saying anything of substance. It's rare to get him on an actual phone call. This is his way of connecting with a variety of women while he pursues the one most open to having sex. He keeps the door open with an occasional "hey." Don't deal with men who text occasionally without making their intentions clear.

> He sends you deep, lengthy texts with long conversations every day or every other day. He loves to FaceTime after work. He is curious about your life and says a lot of the right things. You begin to catch feelings based on your texts although there is no actual relationship, commitment, or even a first or second meeting. What you should do is talk more than text. Don't allow him to take up blocks of your day with texts and calls. Never devote time and emotional energy towards a man who is not consistently meeting with you in person.

> Avoid men who are separated, in unhappy relationships, still seeing their ex, or are "about to

break things off." You should also avoid men who believe in "just seeing where things go," say, "let's flow," or say, "I don't like when people pressure me for an answer/relationship/commitment."

➤ Avoid men who openly look at other women in front of you. Men are visual, but should not be disrespectful.

➤ Avoid men who yell at you or others, give you the silent treatment, only talk about themselves, threaten to leave, get upset when you are busy, pressure you for sex, or avoid doing basic acts of kindness towards you.

➤ Avoid men who "turn the tables" or "have to go" when you share your concerns or feelings.

➤ Avoid the man who tells you sweet, thought-provoking things, yet does not follow through or keep his word. When it is time to show up or do what he said he wanted to do together, he has an excuse. Avoid men who tell you lies. If he lies, he is not the man God has for you!

➤ Avoid men who disappear for days at a time or who can rarely be accounted for. If you are in a relationship, avoid men who consistently tell you they didn't get your text or call because they "fell asleep" or "lost track of time" or similar excuses. There's a difference between being busy and being a ghost.

➤ Avoid men who ask for nude pictures or who try to sext. Once you start, it is hard, if not impossible, to get him to talk about much of anything else.

➤ Avoid men who send you nude or sexually explicit pictures. He has one thing on his mind and is not interested in a committed relationship with a queen.

> Avoid men who push for a committed relationship too soon. Some men just want you to exclusively date them, while they continue dating whomever they please. Do not commit to a relationship until he demonstrates his character through actions.

Dating Mindset #6: Don't ignore red flags.

Many women have spotted inconsistencies, lies, and communication issues yet still hold on to the relationship because she doubts her instincts. Sometimes a woman wants to see the good in the other person so badly that she will sacrifice herself in the process. Other times, the pain of starting over, or being alone makes a woman choose to remain engaged in a relationship that is full of red flags. Sometimes a woman feels self-conscious about her age, about being divorced, or being a single mother. These factors can weigh heavily on a woman who decides to stay with a man who doesn't treat her well.

Much of this can be avoided by:

Working on yourself and doing the work to heal from anxiety, divorce, loneliness, childhood trauma, and abandonment issues.

Engaging in regular exercise like stretching, working out or bike riding is great for confidence boosting and overall well-being. (See chapter six for more information on the importance of your physical health)

> Staying connected to God and leaning on the Holy Spirit for wisdom. You definitely need wisdom when dating, however, if you're dating an older man (5-20 years older) or someone who has been with a lot of women, you need to be particularly discerning. Keep in mind that he has experiences and ideas

that you probably haven't been exposed to yet. Your feelings are more likely to get involved as he drops some advanced techniques on you and treats you in a manner you haven't yet experienced with men your own age. You need wisdom or you could easily get carried away by what is "new." Just remember that new to you, doesn't mean new to him. "If any of you lacks wisdom, you should ask God who gives generously to all without finding fault and it will be given to him" (James 1:5).

➤ Choosing a godly man. There will be issues if the man you're dating is going to the strip club, smoking weed for recreation, excessively drinking alcohol, gambling, watching pornography, and staying connected to activities that fuel his lusts and lifestyle as a player or hustler. If he isn't motivated to change due to an inner conviction that the previous lifestyle is wrong, what will stop him from going back to his old ways after you two have been together for a while? You should not accommodate a sinful lifestyle in order to have a relationship with him.

➤ Not giving second, third and fourth chances. You've all heard the saying: "Fool me once, shame on you. Fool me twice, shame on me." Be discerning about whom you give a second chance.

➤ Choosing a man's character over his income. The most empowering gift you can give yourself is to be honest with yourself. Sometimes, you may be attracting a certain type of man because you value the perks that come with his status, title, and level of affluence more than you value whether he is a moral and decent person or not. The thought of being connected to a high-level man is more attractive than having a man with an average job and no title. Many a king has been overlooked because he did not drive up in the "right" car.

➤ Following Dating Mindset #2.

Go Deeper

1. Here are examples of online resources if you are looking for professional mental health support and guidance: BetterHelp Online Counseling, Soul Injury through Opus Peace, and Thrive Online Community through the Marriage Recovery Center. What does your own search reveal?

2. What can you do to create a relationship based on more than sexual attraction?

3. Make friendship the foundation for your relationship. This takes time. So, within your committed relationship, go on weekly dates and stay connected by phone and text in order to get to know each other. Practice going on inexpensive dates that don't break either of your bank.

4. Make sure to avoid activities that are considered husband or wife duties. Those include sex, living together, sharing a business, bills, pets and having babies.

If you had a positive experience reading this book ... I humbly ask you to share your review on my page at Amazon.com.

On social media tag me: @BishopDSBrister

#99andFine

Thank you!

NOTES

NOTES

NOTES

NOTES

NOTES

Made in the USA
Coppell, TX
30 April 2021

54756488R00069